What It Means To Be Happy

What It Means To Be Happy

Poems

Gary Margolis

GREEN WRITERS PRESS | *Brattleboro, Vermont*

Green Writers Press is a Vermont-based publisher whose mission
is to spread a message of hope and renewal through the words and
images we publish. Throughout we will adhere to our commitment to
preserving and protecting the natural resources of the earth. To that
end, a percentage of our proceeds will be donated to environmental
activist groups. Green Writers Press gratefully acknowledges support
from individual donors, friends, and readers to help support the
environment and our publishing initiative.

Giving Voice to Writers & Artists Who Will Make the World a Better Place

Green Writers Press | Brattleboro, Vermont
www.greenwriterspress.com

ISBN: 979-8-9876631-4-1

COVER ART: "Boston Common at Twilight,"
Museum of Fine Arts. Boston. Childe Hassam.

THE PAPER USED IN THIS PUBLICATION IS PRODUCED BY MILLS COMMITTED
TO RESPONSIBLE AND SUSTAINABLE FORESTRY PRACTICES.

for Stuart Bicknell and Nan Carey,
Sue and Jim Shaw

"Walls of ivy, paths of beauty . . ."

"New Hampton, fair New Hampton . . ."

Contents

1

2

3

4

1

Between You and Me

Nothing might come
between you and me.
Like the earth

passing
between the moon
and the sun.

We'll have our dark days,
a promise I can make
to the stars.

And the minutes,
sometimes
the years, it takes

to apologize.
For the light
to return

to our eyes.
Getting up early
to star gaze.

Rising, we like to say
to each other.
When we're aligned.

When there's nothing
and love
between us.

Earthlings

from here it appears
you're in more trouble than you know
what to do with.

If we thought it would do any good,
we'd send one of our gods to help you
straighten yourselves out.

Even when we pledged not to intervene.
To let your desire and nature
run its own course.

We'd be remiss not to say we survived
ourselves. Without saying anything more
about this.

Some mystery's good.
Some not so good.
Time isn't on your side no matter

what your human being
Einstein thought.
We learned he was almost hit by one

of your cars, one morning,
in Princeton, New Jersey.
Imagine what a loss that would've been

for chalk and blackboards and relativity.
We have our own brilliant heroes.
In fact, you can order one on Amazon.

That dry riverbed in the middle of your planet.
Where the shamans once harvested
their plants.

Knowing the lives they could save
and the trees.
By going into trance

and chanting. Looking to the stars
and the dark, secret notes
we are sending.

What It Means To Be Happy

rejoicing in someone else's
happiness. Foregoing a moment

of useless jealousy. Finding meaning
where the trombone comes in.
In Carlos Simon's symphony,

"Amen." Such pleasurable cacophony.
Listening, by chance, one morning,
to the composer's composing

happiness. Including every instrument
and then some. Some you haven't
heard of. Some you have to make up

names for. Given how they crowd
each other out and in.
Like the mass of birds lighting

on the feeder. How hungry,
they bully each other, with their kind
of love. Scattering seed to the ground.

It pleases you to say they'll find it.
When they still feel hungry for you
to see them. To hear their random

symphony. Notes the wind scores
through the nearby branches.
Which make you happy, thinking

of it again. Feeling their sounds
inside your body. Where things don't
quite make sense. Yet mean it.

Origins of Empathy

There's something to say, isn't there,
for having a name, an address, someplace
in the universe.

For having your own aches and heartaches
every day.
To be known for. To go by.

Even when you can feel empathy
for your neighbor who's laid up
in bed with a bad back.

And calls to his wife,
whenever he needs a glass
of water, yesterday's newspaper.

Even when she isn't home
and he needs to imagine her
with him.

Loneliness and fear two heads
of an ancient coin he saved
from a trip he and his wife made,

to Delphi and the oracle.
Who was known for her prophecies
and lies. For the stories

your neighbor told you,
when he was back home.
And the two of you were more alike

than not. Even with all the different places
in the world you still wanted to go.
On your own. Or together.

If you could afford to.
If you wouldn't mind sharing a lifetime
experience. Unique to the two of you.

And the Plains of Marathon,
you're imagining today. Lying
in bed. Wondering what it would take

to roll over without pain.
What it took Phidippides to carry
the general's message.

Without knowing he was running
the first marathon in history.
Without thinking to himself

he was the only person
in the world who could do this.
One step. One heartbeat. At a time.

My Father-in-Law's False Teeth

At 95, my father-in-law still likes
scaring me. Pushing his false teeth
in and out. Grinning like a bear

on Halloween. Next week's Thanksgiving,
here in half of North America.
I hope he keeps his teeth in

for his great grandchildren
and me. For the stuffing
and mashed potatoes, going

with my mother-in-law's famous
venison gravy. Soft things.
For his plastic teeth. His plate,

he says it's called. An old word
in his dog-eared dictionary.
He's still reading. As if he's working

his way through a turn-of-the century
novel. Looking forward, as he's used
to doing, to the next five years,

day-to-day, week-to-week, year-to-year.
One piece of cake to another.
One slice of pie for each day of his life.

And hers. My mother-in-law,
Barbara, who's as close to God as anyone.
Sitting next to her husband, Richard.

Who, in this family, we call Dede.
For all the good deeds in his life he did
and does, you could say.

Filling the feeder with sunflower seeds
for the black-capped chickadees.
Leaving his teeth in until Christmas.

Circadian

Sometime, long ago, the universe promised
your street a symphony
of insects. An oversized section

of strings. Wings for bows.
The space between buildings
a chamber for a city

of sleepless singers.
Someone, not you, would call
a plague.

If it weren't for their constant
singing, droning. If a less beautiful
word is needed.

Although droning is more accurate
and beautiful.
If you want to call this tinnitus

a symphony of growing
older. In this ear
of the universe.

These stars in the trees,
Scratching and hissing.
Usually late in the afternoon.

Until late into the evening.
When more silence is needed.
More singing.

Back then.
Back there.
In the beginning.

When you're done living in your body

my granddaughter asks me,
what will you do
with your clothes, your riding
lawn mower?

Where will you go?

Can I have your stamps
and coins?
The turkey feathers
in your hat?

Your autographed baseballs?
The letters you keep
in a box?

I don't know what I'll do
with my things
after I'm done living
in my body,
I say.

Trying to say anything
a nine-year-old
can understand.

About dying.
To claim
in her own words.

Imagining a body
can be through with us.

We can be done living
in our bodies.

But not with our beautiful,
useful and useless
things.

Which, even at her age,
she knows
I can pass on.

Chagall's Stained Glass at the Border

Grandfather keeps an antique
saber, rattling
in the attic.

Nana says it smells
to high heavens.
Like a rotting pastrami

sandwich.
I don't want to argue
with them.

Given what's going on
outside Kiev.
Near the shtetl

they escaped from.
A chandelier rattling
in their wagon.

The village fiddle
player rising.
Their cow refusing

to jump.
I leave to you
to guess

from where to where.
Who it was painting her
into his stained glass

window.
Never art for art's sake.
Or an advertisement.

Glass,
some light could make
its way through,

Which is why
grandfather tells me
he saves his sword.

The curved one
with the jeweled,
bloody handle.

He can hold,
wrap his hand around.
When he has to.

Mower's Symphony #8

No one told you it's too hard
to get Beethoven's Symphony #8
out of your head. Walking

behind your ancient push mower.
The blades spinning like notes.
The clippings, a deaf tympani.

Not that you should make
too much of a comparison
between what he heard

in his mind and wrote
with his pen. Letting the notes fly
like swallows eating their fill

of mosquitos, their fill of invisible
thoughts. You love mowing,
you said, because it's monotonous.

A mower's metronome.
Giving you time to contemplate
what you hear in your headphones.

The pauses. The rests. The stops.
A love that almost feels like exercise,
without having to work out.

When you hear yourself humming
one of Beethoven's phrases,
over and over again.

Back and forth across the lawn,
your staves.
Eight rows, *allegro vivace.*

Eight rows, *allegretto scherzando.*
Eight rows of not having to think
anything at all.

Our Class with Yevtushenko

Putin's sitting at the end
of my couch this morning.
I ask him if he's read the poetry

of Yevgeny Aleksandrovich Yevtushenko.
Who visited my class
in Middlebury, Vermont

in the last century.
Who told my students,
to think of their poems as bales

of hay they could throw into the air
of the field. So they can fall apart.
So they could see the flowers

and barbed wire. At the same time.
We took turns going around
the class, reading our poems to him.

Pausing, to see what his eyes thought.
What he was making of our words.
At the end, he said, Listening to you

is like looking into a pail
of fresh milk. Scraping thick
cream from the top.

Which is more generous than I can
remember. It was so long ago,
enemy countrymen were about

to become neighbors. Tyrants,
appeared in dreams, sitting
on couches. And then

the bell rings. The wind
inside, shuffling,
casting our unwritten poems.

How It Was We Looked Ahead

Early on, we expected a tenor to step out
on his balcony to sing to his neighbors.
After work, a parade, a peloton

of cyclists pedaling through the streets,
saluting the front line workers.
Looking up to those of us

well enough to step out
onto our patios,
waving our handkerchiefs.

Later on, a pod of children would
gather in the square
to sing the anthem, show us

they were healthy enough
to hold their hands over their hearts.
Weeks and months passed, getting on

towards winter. Rain ripped
the leaves off again. With the help
of the wind. A few of us felt safe

enough to gather in the stairwells,
sharing puzzles and survival stories.
What we were doing to make

time pass like a movie. To begin
to imagine our new lives.
What we would miss.

What habits we would take with us.
Not knowing
what to do without them.

How they had become essential parts
of our days. From one side of the street
to the other.

Apartment to apartment.
Shouting, as if we were singing.
Throwing baseballs and ornaments.

From window to window.
Things that showed we cared.
Many of us were still here.

X-ing days off our calendars.
Remembering how it was
we looked ahead.

Not Making the Postseason

Some go back to their islands.
Some to their childhood farms.
A few linger in the parking lot

saying goodbye. Looking back
to the stanchions of lights.
The left field wall.

Disappointment as strong
as a flat beer. No one to blame
but themselves and the front

office. Those men sitting
in chairs in front of computers.
The owners somewhere
on their boats in the storm-

wrecked Caribbean. Our star
shortstop probably won't
be here next year.

And a bench of bullpen relievers.
Given how terrible they pitched
in the clutch.

When all we needed
was a few more runs.
Enough to make temporary winners

of them and us.
Enough to keep them here. Late
into October. On the edge

of winter. When here, in Boston,
we've learned, over time,
to move on. To dream of

spring. Somewhere, down there,
in Florida. Sometime in March.
When we're still plowing out.

Hoping there's a boy
in the Dominican oiling his glove.
Dreaming of us.

Your Bucket List

One take-off and landing.
Riding on the wing
of a hummingbird.

Conducting the Boston Pops
on the Esplanade, waving a straw
baton.

Kissing your feet.
Waking up
with a hint

of amnesia.
Drinking what the gods drink.
Letting the tapping sparrow in.

Rising to the occasion.
Sunning on the deck
of a listing ship.

Listening to The Sound
of Silence
in Central Park.

Climbing a rope ladder.
Looking into a mirror,
seeing the face

of a French Bulldog.
Taking my time.
Watching the hands

of my mother's clock.
Sitting on a bench
in a dugout

chewing ambrosia.
Forgetting what there is
to leave out.

2

Freak Storm

Still a giant surprise
when snow drifts the fields
into dunes.

When the plow skis
the road again.
Nothing I'd call

more unusual.
Isn't this what we expect
at the end

of March?
Early flowers,
A bluebird, anxious

to start
nesting.
Nothing I'd call

weirdly out
of place.
Even when I have

to find my car
somewhere
out there

in the swirling,
leafless
shadows.

Which doesn't make me
too much of a freak,
seeing what I see

in the humped-up mounds
of snow.
Remembering,

with you,
what an honor
to be called

a freak, a long time ago.
When March drifted
into April.

When we did everything
we could to stop
the war.

Far Out

Janis Joplin said this is far out,
man.
Pointing to the globs

of colored ink,
on a screen behind her
band.

Like my mind,
she'd be likely to have said.
Not living long enough.

To see today's farthest out
galaxies. Those miraculous
swirls and specs,

the technology
of infrared makes visible
to us.

Lying in bed. Checking
our screens.
For any message from

far away. Out there.
Beyond our dreams.
Of stepping back

to the Start of Everything.
To the night in Buffalo,
at UB, Janis and her Holding Company

held us in ecstasy.
Blew our minds.
When the feeling in her throat broke

free.
And we were taken back.
To what we didn't know

we'd come to hear. To see
Time made visible.
Stars, our love could make.

Shouting with Kindness

for Jerry Stern (1925-2022)

There are poets, like Jerry Stern, who connect
all the invisible dots of the world. I know
you could too if you looked across the road

every morning, bending down to tie your shoes.
Jerry loved comedians who could stand up
and sit down. Who spent summers on the Borscht

Circuit in the Himalayas. My father told me
if I kept speaking out, I'd be accused of having
a big mouth. And wouldn't stand a chance

of climbing an off-limits mountain.
Or becoming a stand-up kind of guy.
That's why I love writing poetry, sitting

in my chair, longer than my back
and legs can stand. Summers, my grandmother
used to leave Cleveland and my grandfather.

Head to the Poconos and cook for all
the bar mitzvah boys and their families.
Recipes only cooks for the Czars knew.

She said, what else is new. Whenever we wanted
to make more of her memory than she thought
was good for us.

Whenever we wanted to know her
secret ingredients. And a few punchlines.
Then came the war and men on both sides

of the road who wanted to keep the Holocaust
a secret. Men who made other men, women
and children tie the commandant's shoes.

If they wanted to live a longer life.
For a few minutes. Stew in their own juices.
A phrase, I'm asking you, my world,

to say in the lost, forgetful tongue
of Yiddish. Say with all of our big mouths.
To go out shouting with kindness.

When We Were Dating

My wife enjoys walking into our bedroom,
after her walk, when I'm half-awake.
And reporting to me the shadows

she's seen in the field at dawn.
I like pretending I'm still asleep.
And whatever she's seen appears

in my dream. I might tell her.
I might keep to myself.
She knows me well enough to know

when I'm faking. Like I did, when I was
twelve and didn't want to wake up,
get dressed and walk to school.

When I told my mother I had
a bad dream. And couldn't tell
what that sound was in my closet.

The shadow I could feel
under my bed. My mother was known
for her love and her drinking.

Some mornings giving in to me.
Most of the time not.
Telling me to get up. Get dressed.

Make my own breakfast.
Which I never mentioned
to my wife when we were dating.

And I was prone to making things
up. But not my breakfast.
That I could hear every word

she says to me, with my head
under the covers.
And whatever it was

in the field coming toward her,
standing on two feet,
she could tell me about later.

Forgot Your Password?

At night, I can't remember
the one I chose. Or if
it chose me.

I like seeing if I can make it up
again.
The name of my first dog,

A Boston Terrier, my father called
Beauty.
Maybe you use the numbers

of your house address.
Followed by an exclamation
point.

I do.
At night, it's easy to take myself
back to the street

I grew up on.
212 Clark Road.
Without telling you anything
about it.

Who lived in our attic
to help my mother out.
Who survived a scary

cancer without a number.
Who lived as long
as she could.

Another story for another
poem. Without
an exclamation point.

Without thinking I could
choose a different
mother.

Even when I used
to tell her, my real mother
wouldn't do what she did.

Wouldn't forget the name
she gave me.
After an afternoon of hard

drinking.
Before my father got home
late from work.

At the door,
asking for our family's
secret password.

Mother-in-Law Astronaut

My mother-in-law, 94, goes in
and out, sleeping in her favorite
chair. By the window, looking

out to the creek. Sometimes
geese land there. In sight
of her. Sometimes she's dreaming

of them. And her husband,
napping next to her.
They like to joke, tell funny

stories, when they're awake
at the same time. Teasing,
asking who's half-way

to heaven. Who's half-way,
down the stairs to the basement.
Where they still keep every tool

in the world. Two pairs of waders.
And a raft of paperback books.
Baba, we call her, reads and rereads.

Saying the second time around
is better. Almost like new, she says.
Having forgotten most of the details

that make her happy again.
That make good use of her mind
and heart. Science fiction novels,

mostly, if you knew her. Beyond
what I'm writing, you'd understand
how she might be the first mother-in-law

NASA would consider sending
on their rocket to Mars. Or at least
to land on the moon.

Taking one giant step for mankind.
One for the geese, honking for her
to come out to read to them.

Strumming the Mask Mandate

I may be the only one
wearing a mask
into the barbecue joint.

Walking to the counter
to pick up my take-out.
Like a gopher tortoise

climbing out of her tunnel.
To eat her dinner
leaves. Head back down

after she's stuffed herself silly.
After she's slipped off
her shell, climbed into

something more comfortable.
That's what they do down there
away from us. Inside their burrows.

Make up their own rules.
Kick back. Listen to a little
Kenny Chesney.

While the rest of us
stand in line. Wondering,
worrying if we'll come down

with it. Cough ourselves
to death. Pretend some velvet
art on the wall will save us.

The portrait of the owner
winning an award for serving
his one millionth pulled pork
sandwich. To a customer

like me, who drives all night
from Vermont.
To lower my mask.

Use one of his award-winning
toothpicks. Later back
in my RV, trying to get

some sleep.
Like a tortoise, closing her
triple-lidded eyelids.

One for the sun.
One for the moon.
One for my man, Kenny.

Zooming into Your Classroom

Thank you for your questions.
For stepping this close
to the screen.

Saying your name.
In front of your teacher,
my daughter.

I'll call Ms Moulton.
On this more formal
occasion.

When did you write
your first poem?
A moment ago, I say.

Why don't you rhyme
more often?
Your teacher is my

daughter, I say, day
after day.
What's your favorite

device?
Mine's alliteration,
Mr. Margolis.

I'd have to say the line
break. Knowing where
and when to let a line

turn its corner.
To discover what I didn't
know is there.

Like the bear I saw loping
in my backyard.
Stopping to eat a city

of dandelions.
Before disappearing
into the back

woods. You can tell
I like making things
up inside

the mind of a poem.
Comparing things
to each other, at first,

that don't seem
to go together.
Your teacher, standing

near you, probably
taught you that is called
a simile, a metaphor.

Fancy words.
For the love we feel
inside the heart

of a third grade
classroom.
June 6, 2022.

In Lincoln Elementary School.
In Chicago. In the United States
of America.

On planet Earth.
Our spot.
In the zooming in Universe.

Parade

I wouldn't mind sitting next to
Miss Vermont,
in the back seat of her convertible.

Crowned. And waving my right
hand at the crowd.
Something she seems to have

picked up from Queen Elizabeth
and the Queen Mother.
Swiveling her wrist. As if she'd

grown up in front of a mirror
in her father's milking parlor.
Waving to the cows

standing in their gowns,
in their stanchions.
No one knows if she'll be beautiful

and cool enough,
when she leaves our state and enters
the national competition.

For now, she's our smart, beautiful
princess and queen, young woman
of the barn and milking machines.

Who am I to judge how far
she'll go in this contest, this life?
And for that matter me,

trying to copy her.
Throwing colored pieces
of hard candy to the curb.

Where a herd of girls
are sitting. Breaking rank
with their mothers. Running

into the street to win
a handful of them.
As if this was Halloween

and not Memorial Day.
The washed fire trucks,
 across from us.

Firefighters dressed
in their dress uniforms.
And not one veteran

from the world wars,
as there used to be.
Marching. Sitting

in their cars. Saluting
the sirens. Flirting,
with Miss Vermont.

One of the great freedoms
they fought, they served for.
I enjoy myself.

So I can sit next to
Miss Vermont.
A man wise enough

to wear a crown.
To slip into my barn boots.
My golden slippers.

Their Guns

I'm planning on strolling over
to the bodybuilder, flexing
his biceps in the mirror.

Requesting he not use
the f-word so often.
To impress the woman,

it seems, on the other side
of the gym. Looking into
her mirror. To gain

the attention, too,
of the young man, casting
f-bombs, whenever he fails

to snatch and jerk, to beastie
up his barbell weight.
A phrase I'd only use inside

my amateur poem. And not say
to his face. Although
I'm guessing he'd be pleased.

Referred to as a f'ing
beast. Happy to feel me
trying to press, to throw my weight

around. Feel me, another
phrase you're likely to hear
more often now, in the streets.

When men are emotional.
Showing off their guns,
stretching their cotton T-shirts.

Their hard muscles glistening
like motherfucking
rifles.

The Dying

Sometimes they wait for us.
Sometimes they can't help
themselves.

Time's on their side
and ours.
You'll try to arrive in time.

Look into her eyes.
Hold her hand.
Surrounded by family,

a phrase an obituary
writes.
Sometimes ahead of time.

No matter who's there.
A nurse. A custodian.
A visitor walking by.

Who might have to stand in
for you. When it's time
to say good-bye.

Words your father never said.
Not letting his feelings rise.
For you to see.

Or anyone
who happened to be
nearby.

"Seeking Right-Handed Black Gloves"

If I didn't know better, I'd say Pablo
Neruda's my next door neighbor.
Given the above request she's making

of our neighborhood. In Front Porch Forum.
I don't know how she knew
I'd been thinking of writing an ode

to all the lost gloves here
in Vermont. In the lost and found
at ski areas. In school bins, outside

the doors of cafeterias.
Even in the former Ladies' room
in Burlington, at the Flynn Theater.

Where the signs have been changed
to accommodate anyone who isn't afraid
to lose, leave a glove behind.

Silk or wool. Depending on the matinee.
Who that afternoon's performance
might appeal to.

Who might respond to my appealing
neighbor. Who, like me, doesn't want to
write half an ode. To a state

of left-handed gloves. Roaming the back
roads, like hounds, searching
for a right-handed bear.

Dog-sitting

When my wife leaves me
for a few days home
with the dog, it's all

we can do not to stretch out
on the couch together
with our favorite snacks,

flip through the channels
for a show we both like.
A documentary from *National*

Geographic or a rerun of
National Lampoon.
Together we sing, we howl

the National Anthem
and hold our breaths
when the Blue Angels,

fly, wing-to-wing, over
a stadium. Such patriots
we are at this distance.

Without having to belong
to a party. Letting the dishes
pile up in the sink, our beds

go unmade. Even watching
a few racy cartoons,
neither of us has to own

up to. Such trust we feel,
looking into each other's
eyes. Knowing there are

secrets that are ours
to keep. Like bones.
Like candy wrappers

I can't remember hiding.
Or that flag with an embroidered
Pug I pledge my allegiance to.

Each night my wife's away.
Doing what wives do,
when there isn't a dog

to walk, a husband asleep
on the couch, in the kennel
of their bedroom.

3

At the Pain Clinic

Please don't assume the speaker
is speaking or writing about himself.
Or there's anything unusual

about sitting in a waiting room,
reading a magazine with a roomful
of other men and women.

Even if sitting too much and too long
is likely what's brought them here.
Or a lifetime of hunching

over a desk, looking up to a screen.
Raking a yard full of leaves.
Angles, apparently, the body,

yours and mine, is never meant for.
Even when I said I wasn't going
to mention myself.

As if I was also the speaker
of this poem.
Waiting my turn to be tested,

diagnosed
with a condition
I've never dreamed of.

Dreamed, not as in sleeping.
But more in imagining
what my body comes to.

A model of a skeleton.
A list of possible injections.
Even if saying this, and I am

the speaker, is going too far,
getting ahead of myself.
And you. Even if we see

ourselves in the waiting room.
As someone we once knew.
Someone we might have

even gone out with. Although,
the speaker should probably
say dated. Dating himself and her.

In Front of "The Last Supper"

Certainly you're not the first Jew,
to walk in from the square.
Into the convent, Saint Apollonia.

To stand in front of Jesus
and friends, sitting at a long supper
table. Del Castagno brushed

into the wet, drying wall.
Even now, you're amazed how
friendly and relaxed they appear

after all these frozen-in-time years.
How little and more has changed.
The memory of nuns kissing

his sandy feet.
As if Jesus had just
walked back from the sea,

the beach with his friends.
Not Christ yet. Or betrayed.
Which was part of the plan.

To sustain a wound.
From a good friend.
To love him anyway.

To not turn away from
yourself.
Even if you're the only Jew

here this Sunday morning.
With a guidebook in your hand.
Assigning names to faces.

Feeling what one nun felt.
Looking at Jesus. Wanting more
than anything to tell her best friend.

I Am the Constable

When I call the police
to report a herd of horses
grazing my backyard,

they tell me to call
my local constable.
That's me! I say.

Although I've never lassoed
anything.
Ridden to a high pasture

to round up a stable
of studs and mares.
Or tried to coax them back

with my can of grain.
Or by writing a poem.
Reading the first draft

to them.
Hoping they'd amble over,
prick up their ears.

Catch a mustang phrase.
Enough to please
a thoroughbred. If not

these rodeo and summer
camp horses. I learn break
loose. Because they can

jump fence lines.
Graze, from field-to-field.
Before the heavy snows arrive.

Before anyone calls me,
our town's poet-constable.
Expecting I'd know how

to approach them.
At least the black and white one.
Without her bolting,

kicking up her heels.
Showing me what I never learned.
What I could do.

Waking, at dawn.
Dreaming.
Seeing real horses

composing themselves
into stanzas
on my lawn.

Blues Bar on Jefferson Avenue in Buffalo

What we were thinking, thinking
we could walk into a blues bar
on Jefferson Avenue, in Buffalo.

A trio of white boys.
Trying to look like we belonged.
That it didn't matter,

when one of us, me, spilled a beer
by mistake on a patron,
sitting at his table.

The music stopped for a beat.
All eyes on us. Each of us
realizing what could happen.

A fight? A moment
of grace? A future of something
worse. I made my best

apology. For thinking I could
just walk into the community
for a few hours. Leave.

Make my mistake. And be
forgiven for it. At least not
beaten up.

Humiliation being
one punch I could take.
And never forgetting

the memory of that night.
I was told to stay
cool. Everything would be all right.

We all could ride the midnight train
to Georgia. Sit on the dock
of the bay together.

Elsie's Special

Maybe there's a sandwich shop
near you. You can walk to.
Like mine, once in Harvard Square.
Within walking distance

of the bronze statue of John Harvard.
On whose leg, if I tell the truth,
I keyed my name into,
To make it seem, I was one

of them—tweed-suited, Meerschaum-
pipe-smoking. And not just
who I was. A boy from Brookline,
across the Charles. Trying to crowd in

at the counter. Shouting my order
with the confidence of a coxswain,
crossing a loud, finish line.
A would-be poet, who couldn't stand it,

when Gordon Cairnie, true owner
of the Grolier Book Store (all poetry,
around the corner) yelled at me
to hold a book with two hands.

If I needed to hold it at all.
Never again eat a sandwich,
in his sight. Even if it was his friend Elsie's
Elsie's Special. Roast beef with her

secret dressing on a roll. Handed to you
with her special love.
Meant for anyone who didn't mind
standing in that crush

of students and professors.
Cobblestone street cleaners.
Hard hat workers.
High-schoolers skipping class.

Like me, tamping
tobacco into my pipe.
Reading Rilke in translation.
Saving half my sandwich for later.

As if I knew what I was doing.
And could write it down
in lines for you. The truth
inside my lies.

Center Court

You can't tell me you didn't twirl,
too, your last day of work
at the office.

Didn't imagine yourself dressed
in a gown. With sequined hair,
spinning at center court.

Waving to your students,
as if they were fans
in the Arthur Ashe stadium.

Ready to give you
their standing ovation.
Whether you won or lost.

Whether the last ball you hit
stayed in, went flying out.
Beyond all praise and thought.

Even a queen has to pack it in.
Think of herself as you.
As one of her fans coming

to the end of their first,
their second service.
With so many jobs

where you do everything
needing to be done.
Repairing a net.

Washing a wristband.
Without anyone noticing.
Without anything added

to your check. Enough
to pay for going to
a hairdresser once a month.

Having an artist paint
your nails. Paying a dancer
to teach you to twirl.

On your last day of work.
In the heart
of Flushing Meadows.

On Billy Jean's court.
Coming to net.
In Queens, New York.

In the Voting Booth

In Cornwall, my small town
in Vermont, a precinct of deer
and leaves, I like to think

of my neighbors, likely
to volunteer for anything.
Coming to our town hall,

to set up enough easily
taken down booths.
I like to think of

as little puppet theaters,
cabanas for changing
our government every

two and four years.
Our own version of voting
democracy. Where,

if you lived here and stood
in the booth next to me, trying
to decide who'd make a good

watcher-of-fence-posts, counter-
of-coal, even a next, best president,
it wouldn't surprise you to hear one of us

asking, from booth-to-booth,
Charlie, who are you voting for?
How's your good wife?

Did you get your deer?
Questions, I like to think,
whoever it is next to you answers.

Privacy, a luxury, native and flat-
lander alike, we give up, for the beauty
of stepping outside in the coming

snow. Leaving tracks with our boots
and poles, the skis on our snowmachines.
The privilege of feeling the plow

in the middle of the night, shaking
the house. Like votes from the heavy
branches. Falling. Making a country again.

Children's Hospital

The boy in the bed next to me,
waiting, too,
for his surgery.

We say our names
to each other.
In the dawning.

When the nurse arrives
to calm me, to hold me.
To tie me down

with her shot.
To wheel me
down the hallway.

Through the double doors.
To lift me
onto

a table.
To be sacrificed,
I'm too young

to think.
Just feel.
Seeing the gloved hands.

The mask.
The light adjusted
above me.

Annual Exam

You know you're healthy, at least healthier,
when your doctor tells you more
about his annual exam than yours.

Reads you his print-out of his lab results.
Asks for your opinion whether he should get
the latest booster shot.

Not sure himself what good it would do.
Even if he wouldn't say that to just anybody.
Even when it's your body you're here for.

More than once-a-year. And not his.
Even when you wish him well.
Hope he'll be here in a year.

For your next annual exam.
Yours and his. And neither of you
will outlive each other. Come

to the same conclusion.
You really wouldn't want it
any other way. At this point

in your healthy, dwindling life.
Wouldn't want to tell your whole
medical history.

To a boy, an intern in a white coat,
sharing with him why you used to speak
into your late doctor's stethoscope.

So he could hear every word
you wanted him to hear.
Why at this point in your life

you needed to spend more time
talking with him.
About the Soul and Time.

Your bedroom window.
The fields beyond.
Why that deer is lying down.

New Routine

Some mornings my wife brings the dog
to me while I'm still in bed.
He seems uncomfortable, so far out

of his element. Sleeping in front
of the fireplace.
Curling up in a sunspot,

he spends most of his day in.
Until he finds the scent
of my wife, his true, best friend.

Lingering on a pillow.
And seems more at peace with himself
and me.

Not as agitated or anxious
to be any place else.
On earth. Or farther away.

Making a star of himself.
Somewhere in our galaxy.
My wife said I'll need to walk him.

Take him out. Get some fresh air.
Not spend all day in the kennel
of our bed.

While she's gone, at work.
At this point in our lives
making a living

for the three of us.
Walking home in the dark
at the end of her day.

Calling for one of us.
Like my father said,
to rise and shine.

My Sister's Dress

One night, my sister away,
for an overnight,
I dressed up in her fancy dress.

Smudged her lipstick
on my boring lips.
I was alone. We shared a room.

Mother and father slept
across the hall.
They couldn't tell

what I was doing.
I was her. She wasn't me.
I swayed like our street's

empty trees.
I felt what it was like
to take the lead.

Leaned in to kiss her.
To kiss the air.
Knowing she wasn't there.

Until she was. Waltzing
through the door.
Saying she missed me.

Her friend was boring.
What was I doing anyway,
without her. Dressed up

as the most beautiful girl
in our attic room.
In her party shoes.

The pair she never told me
were really ours.
Were never meant

to be taken out
of the box,
stepped out in.

Proposal

I propose to my granddaughter
that for every hour
she's off her phone, she's reading

one of my poems, reading
a Russian novel,
I'll donate a dollar

to her college savings account.
To the Ukrainian children's relief fund.
In between texts, she tells me

school's starting in a few weeks.
And she'll be reading more books
than her shelves can hold.

On the bus. Under her covers.
In between apps, she searches
for a few facts of the authors

she's reading. For a book report
due in December.
When the power's bound to be out,

no way to connect to WiFi,
to a satellite.
When her phone's as useful

as a bookmark from a bookstore
in town, going out of business.
I tell her it's our duty to keep

open. Anything we can do
to save a library.
To stop the war.

King's Pen

Not surprising when the king blurts out,
this stinking pen.
When the ink leaks out all over

his white-gloved hands.
When he's trying his best
to go from prince

to king.
Sign his signature
in the ancient book

of queens and kings.
Knights who stamped
their bloody thumbs

on the pages. Given
so few of them could write
their names. In anything

but blood. From a stag.
A doe. An insubordinate.
This first morning an aide

makes a human mistake.
Not rising, before dawn
to fill the little well

beforehand. Write his own
name in invisible ink
in the great book--

for practise--to see
if the bloody ink stays.
Doesn't run or smudge.

Won't be the cause
of the new king
having a bad day.

Over the Holidays

Don't think no one's counting.
The number of drinks. The handful
of ice cubes clinking. Their melting

diamonds. Such vigilance
over the coming holidays.
Someone has to do it, you say

to yourself. Slicing the turkey.
Watching, without looking.
Hearing, without listening.

Trying to look inconspicuous.
As if you're not there.
In sight of the empty bottles.

As if you don't remember
her slurred words, her off-kilter
dresses. All the excuses

for going to bed early.
Retiring. Leaving the table
for us, to clean off the dishes.

Make up our own versions
of how wonderful it is
to be together.

Minute of Silence

for Butch Varno, in memoriam

We stand for a minute
   of silence.
To let his name
   return
from there
   across the stadium
to the leaf-painted
   mountains.
Aware there's still
   a game
to play. A half-time
   to wander around
   the tailgating
without him.
   Or stop by his
wheelchair to ask
   how his week's been
in the nursing home
   where he's lived
for so many years.
   The nurses are his
sisters and girlfriends.
   The men on the night shift,
teammates and brothers.
   Until it's time to remember
to watch the game again.
   Time running out
in the fourth quarter.

With a few seconds left
to imagine our hometeam
    scoring. Kicking an impossible
field goal.
    For the sake of the beautiful
fall day here,
    in Vermont.
Across our unlikely
    nation.
For the sake of losing him
    last night. Butch,
who'd do anything
    he could to get us
to overtime.
    To give us a chance
of winning.

4

Writing to the Wind

Let me be one of the first to tell you,
you're a magnificent writer.
I've read your letters, your holiday

cards, your sticky notes.
How you say things in such a caring,
original way. Soft-spoken. Hand-written.

There isn't anyone I know
who wouldn't want to walk
to their mailbox and see an envelope

from you. The mailman dropped off.
Although it's more likely you walked it
over yourself. Wanting to drop it gently,

so no words would be lost. The box,
left open to the snow or rain. Which happens
sometimes, when wind makes its way in.

Wanting to be one of your readers, too.
Which, Peter, I'm happy to say I've been.
On my birthday. On every other occasion

there is for you to express your love
of bees, of sheep, of letters spun into words.
The first page of your story, you can write to the wind.

When the Kreemee Stand Opens

In Vermont, you can tell March
is almost over.
A local owner throws open
her take-out window.

Even when everyone around here knows
April's snow will fill a thousand
village cones.
And some of us waited all winter

for a swirled chocolate and vanilla one.
Dipped in a cloud
of colored sprinkles.
Even when none of us are

counting yet how many e's it takes
to spell Kreemee. And if K
looks better backwards, Russian-style.
If we Vermonters aren't afraid

to hold down a computer key.
To see how many m's it takes
to make a word feel special.
Five or ten. A number

not invented yet.
Like a flavor, half-maple,
(remember the state we're in)
half-venison.

Saving Time

My granddaughter asks me
where does the hour go.
Into earth?

Back to the stars?
She says her friend told her
even Einstein didn't know.

And he was a genius.
An expert on time and space.
And winding back the hands

of his grandfather's clock.
Which lived in his living room.
Chiming away. A relatively

common occurrence then.
When watchmakers were master
carpenters. And artists

painted a moon
rising on the face
of a clock. A mystery,

of course. Even to Albert
and his crazy hair. Who,
it's rumored, jolted himself

once a year. To be reminded
to turn time forward or back.
With his skeleton key.

Depending on what season it was.
He could tell by looking outside
at the flowers and leaves.

At the children
walking to school,
holding each other's hands.

New Country

My friend suggests I use rhyme more
often. He's an old college friend for some reason
I can't recall we called Buffalo. I guess I'll have to ask him

if he remembers why he was tagged with that nickname.
Perhaps in the nick of time. Before he was tagged
with another unforgettable name. Last night,

I could have dreamt we were riding on the plains,
skipping college altogether. Taking a gap year,
it's called now. Working. Traveling. Volunteering.

Reading a book we weren't assigned, in ancient,
rhymed poetry. With rhyming words at the end
of lines. Couplets, sestinas and the impossibly

beautiful villanelle. Maybe he's suggesting
I try writing. If I had more patience and skill.
If my mind worked better, riding in an English saddle.

Roaming is the word I'd use here. More
of how I'm accustomed to following the trail
of blank, free verse. Letting it take me

where it will. Back to the days of yore
in our men's dormitory. In those days
men and women had to live with their own kind.

Their own gender. Impossible to imagine now
with how things have changed. How we probably
wouldn't tag anyone Buffalo.

No matter how much we might have been
teasing or drinking. Micro-aggressing,
the phrase used now. To describe

when you might have been offended
against. Which to my knowledge, in my memory,
we just sucked up. Not wanting to show our pain.

Not wanting to tell anyone of our immigrant,
original beginnings. Somewhere out there
in the middle of our new country.

Under the stars. Lying on a horse blanket.
Strumming a guitar.
And possibly singing.

After a Long Flight

I doubt God would have created potatoes
and pronouns, if They didn't want me
standing in line at Al's French Fries

in Burlington, Vermont. Close to the airport.
My first stop when I fly home to
my Green Mountain state.

Where I doubt many tourists know
in the back room Al keeps a can
of Fancy Grade A syrup.

You can ask for. To pour over your
fries. If you can show them your license,
even if you're not a native Vermonter.

Someone who was born a doubter.
Who could swear God poured gold
from those leaf-painted trees.

When, in March, the temperature rises
and falls overnight, creating the best
sap run. A sweet maple water to boil off

into clouds of Christ. I doubt
you'll believe me when I tell you
one cloud looked so much like Him,

like They, I wanted to call a priest
to prove this. To believe what I was seeing.
Even though I wouldn't say, too,

I see God in everything.
After a long flight. In every pronoun.
In the potato the ground carved into

the face of God. The pleasure I feel
standing in Al's long line. Home
at last. Smothering my fries in my state's

kingdom of maple syrup.
No matter what the doctors nearby
at the medical center tell me isn't

good for me.
No matter how much doubt
there is in the world.

Not Who You Know

Not that I want to name-
drop this early in the morning.
Not that I remember or ever

knew the names of my four
classmates, sitting in SUNY
Buffalo rows. In a trailer

meant more for a building
site in Lackawanna than five
summer school students.

Picking up easy credits
for taking a course he called
"Poets of Despair." Listening

to him recite long passages
from Robinson, Jeffers and Frost.
By heart. Without any notes

he needed to stay sober.
Come to class a summer school
one day at a time. Without telling us

he was a poet. Without including
the names of his prizes in his bio,
he never included in the place

for a brief intro to the instructor
below a course's lengthy description.
Particularly this one, where we'd be

expected to carry our grief
to the poems we heard, we read later,
after work. Two of us working

in the failing steel mills. One leading
tours in the late afternoon
in the Albright Knox Museum.

Across from the bedlam asylum.
I could see from my bedroom window.
Anytime I needed to see why

I was writing a paper for him,
for myself. For Edward Arlington Robinson
who wrote poems for the dead

in his imaginary town.
Where the dead still rise, Wright said.
Without thinking anything of it.

Without mentioning the dead he loved
in his hometown, on the river.
In Martins Ferry, Ohio. Without

quoting his own poems.
Without saying how many pages we had
to write in our final essays.

Extreme Effort

I want to thank everyone of you
in the United States
who made the effort
to travel over the holidays.

Who arranged for your pets
while you were away.
Your cats and tropical fish.
Your hamsters, spinning their wheels.

Who asked a neighbor to take in
your mail. And yesterday's
newspapers. With inserts
announcing their sales.

I want to thank the thieves
who forswore stealing
boxes left by your door.
Taking a few days off

from their thievery.
Letting the gifts pile up,
delivered from warehouses
around the country.

And not from a river
deep in the jungle.
I want to thank, too.
For not giving up.

For refusing to speak
of its soul.
It goes without saying,
I want to express my gratitude

to the workers working overtime.
In the toll booths.
At exits. On bridges.
At the beginnings and ends

of tunnels. In rooms
with so little air.
So grateful for the owners,
who haven't abandoned

their stores. Who stay open
24/7. Even in February
on its intercalary, leap year day.
An extra day, for you,

my citizens, still trying
to get home. To your dogs
and mail. To the memories
of where you've been.

Magenta Moon

R suggests there's nothing
beautiful if I don't have you
to share it with.

There's something beautiful,
otherworldly about the way
he speaks so straightforwardly,

so down-to-earth.
The moon sets in a color
I can't explain.

Magenta comes closest to it.
From here, it appears to be
ten times its usual size.

Like a melon I've never seen.
Filled with summer rain
on the morning horizon.

So beautiful I want to shake you.
Call you to the screen.
If I didn't think what you're dreaming

could be just as beautiful.
Gorgeous even, keeping it
inside yourself. Even

when I sense what R means.
When the two of us look
to an orchard in the sky.

Look to each other,
without having to say
anything.

Carry-on

You're packing to fly
to the gay state
of snorkels and palms.

Forts and manatees.
Seeing how many books
and shorts you can fit into

your carry-on.
After a long winter
of covid and hearings.

The red tide of this war.
Don't think you haven't thought
of canceling your trip,

a few days off.
Staying home. Doing more
with your time

and money. Than sitting,
looking up from your book,
watching the pelicans dive,

smash the waves for fish.
Rise again into their squadrons,
their groups. Drafting the roofs

of condominiums. Rented
to men like you, their girlfriends,
boyfriends and pets.

Including, for free, you'd like
to think, a planeload of refugees.
A few of the thousands

the president pledged
to take in.
With their backpacks.

Their wish to be home.
And not here,
sitting with you,

in the state of Florida.
A stone's throw
from the drawbridge

of St. Augustine.
Ponce-de Leon's gay
fountain of youth.

Lingering

You kiss your wife's best friend
on the cheek. As if
the two of you've agreed

to this. Vowed to greet
each other face-to-face.
To meet after work.

Sometimes you forget
and kiss her on the lips.
And linger longer

than lingerie on a bedroom
hook. Lipstick left on
your white dress shirt.

Dedication

Perhaps to my late father and sister,
my distant grandmother.
To my former girlfriend.

Even if that's likely to start
a riff between me
and my wife.

To my in-laws and their hunting
cabin in the woods.
I wouldn't go there without them.

As dedicated as I am to my city
life.
To not knowing what to do

with a knife and a rifle.
A doe lying on her side.
On second thought, to my favorite

stone.
The one I found underneath another
stone.

And still carry with me. Whenever
I step outside. Whenever
I need a lucky charm. A stone

to skip across a pond.
A piece of the earth to touch
at night.

To my love, my stone.
Might be better for me
to consider in the long run.

Without naming anyone
specifically.
Not my children

or my lifelong friends.
Not my first grade teacher,
my mentor.

Who taught me some names
are meant to go
nameless.

Leading me to ask myself
again.
Why not leave the dedication

page blank?
Like that mirror. That surface
of a pond.

At Your Celebration of Life

You would've gotten a kick
out of how many times the f-word
was used by those closest to you.

Making it seem you were here, too.
And we're sitting around your patio,
drinking a late afternoon beer, sharing

a few off-colored jokes.
The raunchier the better.
Helping us, actually, to have to

imagine the day we can't ask you
to crank up the tunes,
grill the burgers rare.

For God's sake,
not to effing leave us. Now.
Not any day. To tell the drips

and monitors to go the f-
away. To leave you alone
with us. Professor, Executive

VP Cason.
To swear our love
to you. Revel in what

your sergeant said, seeing
a private's rifle jammed.
Fuck this fucking fucker's fucked.

Without knowing how much
you loved parts of speech.
How many international ways

there are to tell cancer
to go fuck itself,
one way and another.

John and Paul

Here they are again,
on film, fooling around
in their makeshift

studio, with George
and Ringo behind them.
Making sounds—any sounds—

before they find the right words.
So not composed, it appeared,
smoking themselves into history.

Making a mess of their old
songs, for the sake of a new
posterity.

Even when Yoko is there, too.
Velcroed to John.
Screaming into a microphone.

When they give her a chance.
When they need to break
for their tea and toast.

Making space, at this point
in the filming, so they could
come together.

For the sake of a song.
If not for each other.
If not for the hope

at this time in their lives,
somehow they can still
get back, get back together.

Virtual Town Meeting

Your town voted down
the proposal to let
the general store sell
legal pot.

You've never been a big fan
of cannabis.
Having once flown
too high.

Having found yourself climbing
the walls
of a strange apartment.
Making love

with a stranger.
Although you love the scent
and music of Marley
and the Dead.

Who filled a field of fans.
Years ago, in an airport
parking lot. Or was that
Vermont's homegrown

Phish? Two memories
you love to confuse.
For the sake of telling
your children.

You still remember idling
after a concert,

bumper-to-bumper. Until
dawn. And the lights

glowing in a nearby barn.
The cows lowing to go out.
Start their long day of grazing.
Filling their bags.

Until it's time to follow
the path back to their stanchions.
Unload themselves, listening,
you want to call it, to the radio

a milking hand propped
on a beer can. A beer brewed
in one of our local breweries.
My town approved.

To build next to
the Little League field.
Where, between innings,
you could grab a beer.

If you were someone who didn't care
what a child, a player might think.
Because there wasn't a rule
or law against it.

Against listening to Kenny Chesney,
one of my favorite island
rum-drinkers, singing
our national anthem.

"Thought Experiment"

after John Koethe

You like thinking of what's false
and true at the same time. The way dusk's
the end of the afternoon and the beginning

of night. Thinking of the invisible
owl and the calls it makes. Somewhere
between a song and a moan. And the silence

you hear between sounds. Which is another
way of telling me you like a full, half-truth.
Leaving me to fill in the rest. Isn't speculation

part imagination, part fact? The two of us not
speaking of how essential the truth is,
when talking about the politics of history,

the reality of science. The innuendos living
in any friendship. Between love's inevitable
pauses. Like that moment you can't tell,

if it's day or night. If that's your heartbeat
or mine. As if that matters as much
as walking into the woods together,

stopping to listen
to the fact of the wind, the lie of the owl
making up its word.

In Blue and Yellow

My granddaughter and I
like texting each other
good-night.

Sending pictures we find
on the Internet.
She's learning French.

I cut and paste all things
Français.
A village with cobbled streets.

A loaf of fresh, French bread.
A red beret, she'd look good in.
Sitting in a café, one day,

studying abroad.
Watching beautiful strangers
walk by, on the Champs-Élysées.

When she's tracing the end
of the other war.
The liberation of cities.

Of survivors of the Holocaust.
Of a few words saved
for the lighting of the

Eiffel Tower again.
Like tonight, she types,
under the image

of La Tour d'Eiffel.
Lit up in blue and yellow.
Colors of the flag

of the Ukrainian exchange
student, she writes,
who sits next to her

in sixth grade.
Who's trying to find
the right words.

Any phrase to speak
for what she's seeing
on the screen, on her phone.

Writing a Poem in Prison

Maybe you're still writing
a sestina. A form for recycling
words and feelings. I wish I could still
sit inside with you, in our guarded

classroom. Locking down your heart's
found words. Writing, really, what you're
feeling. About that morning.
You lost all feeling. For your lying

brother. Lost your mind for the time
it takes to squeeze a trigger. Forgetting,
for the life of you, who was your brother.
The time you're serving for murder.

It feels like it takes a lifetime, you said.
Letting your guard down, to find your heart's
right words. Lying in your cell at night.
Watching the moon silver anything

it can't deliver. Another chance to believe
your brother. Forgetting why it was
you stole his gun. How you weren't taught
to feel what you felt. To write it down.

To Bread Loaf

I don't know how many times
I've come upon your yellow buildings.
Driving home. From the other side
of the mountain. Slowed enough

to see the slow-for-moose sign
and two Conference conferees
walking across Route 125. Oblivious
to me, and, for a moment, to the tinting

maples. The never-changing, slighted
evergreens. So immersed, it seems, in telling
each other how they felt, what they thought
of the last reading. Sitting in the wooden

rows in the Little Theater.
Or a line that suddenly, it appears,
comes to the woman closest to Treman,
A bar of a yellow building.

Where, a would-be writer myself,
I served Bloody Marys. In between readings.
I could tell them so many vodka, tomato juice
stories. And one long, narrative poem

maybe I'll write. To include
Mailer, Crews, and Sexton.
Who dragged on a cigarette longer
than I can remember. The night, after

the last reading of that summer's Conference,
I turned to you in the shade
of the mountain, shaking my made-up
antlers. Saying something about

how easy it seemed, after two weeks
here, sitting and listening, and one night
dancing. To imagine staying
in Maple, one of the yellow buildings.

All winter. With a pen and a notebook.
A loaf of bread. No matter how sentimental
it seems, my mentor said,
Don't be afraid to write it.

Right words come slowly
or early. Like snow in the middle
of August. A shadow stepping out
of the forest.

Acknowledgements

Many of these poems appear, sometimes in earlier versions, on my Facebook page. I am grateful for their readers.

Others are published in the *Addison Independent, Seven Days, Cornwall Newsletter, On the Seawall* and *Vox Populi.*
 "Shouting with Kindness" for Jerry Stern.
 "Minute of Silence" for Richard "Butch" Varno.
 "Writing to the Moon" for Peter Lebenbaum.
 "Magenta Moon" after the work of Rupert Spira.
 "At Your Celebration of Life" for Jeffrey Cason.
 "Thought Experiment" after John Koethe.
 "Writing a Poem in Prison" for the inmates at Great Meadow Correctional Facility.

About the Author

AUTHOR PHOTO BY WENDY LYNCH

GARY MARGOLIS is Emeritus Executive Director of College Mental Health Services and Associate Professor of English (part-time) at Middlebury College. He was a Robert Frost and Arthur Vining Davis Fellow and has taught at the University of Tennessee, Vermont, and the Bread Loaf and Green Mountain Writers' Conferences.

His third book, *Fire in the Orchard* was nominated for the 2002 Pulitzer Prize for Poetry, as well as *Raking the Winter Leaves: New and Selected Poems* in 2010. His poem, "The Interview" was featured on National Public Radio's "The Story." And he was filmed on the Middlebury College campus, reading his poem, "Winning the Lunar Eclipse" for Boston's Channel 5 after the 2003 World Series. In fall 2021, he was Alumni Writer at Bread Loaf, in support of Middlebury undergraduates in residence on the mountain campus. For many years, he has served as the Cornwall, Vermont Town Poet.

Dr. Margolis was awarded the first Sam Dietzel Award for mental health practice by the Clinical Psychology Department of Saint Michael's College and the Counseling Service of Addison County's Wilton W. Covey Community Award in Middlebury, Vermont

His clinical articles have appeared in the *Journal of American College Health, Ladies' Home Journal,* and *Runner's World Magazine.* He has been interviewed for his work with college students by *Time Magazine, ABC,* and *CBS News.*

His memoir is *Seeing the Songs: A Poet's Journey to the Shamans in Ecuador.* Recent books of poems include *Time Inside* and *Museum of Islands: New and Selected Poems.*

CPSIA information can be obtained
at www.ICGtesting.com
Printed in the USA
BVHW041505120623
665618BV00001B/4